DOMINOES

Zombie Attack!

QUICK STARTER   250 HEADWORDS

OXFORD

UNIVERSITY PRESS

Great Clarendon Street, Oxford, OX2 6DP, United Kingdom

Oxford University Press is a department of the University of Oxford.
It furthers the University's objective of excellence in research, scholarship,
and education by publishing worldwide. Oxford is a registered trade
mark of Oxford University Press in the UK and in certain other countries

First published in Dominoes 2013

2017 2016 2015 2014 2013

10 9 8 7 6 5 4 3 2 1

No unauthorized photocopying

ISBN: 978 0 19 424986 7   Book
ISBN: 978 0 19 424959 1   Book and MultiROM Pack
MultiROM not available separately

Printed in China

This book is printed on paper from certified and well-managed sources

ACKNOWLEDGEMENTS

Cover artwork and illustrations by: Nelson Evergreen/The Bright Agency

The series editors wish to express their thanks to Hardy Griffin for his helpful
comments on the story.

The publisher would like to thank the following for their permission to reproduce photographs:
Kobal Collection p25 (Shaun of the Dead film poster/Big Talk/WT 2) OUP p24 (Honeybee/
Photodisc) .

DOMINOES

Series Editors: Bill Bowler and Sue Parminter

Zombie Attack!

Lesley Thompson

Illustrated by Nelson Evergreen

Lesley Thompson was born in Newcastle-upon-Tyne, in the North of England, but she moved to Spain some years ago, and now lives near Alicante. She loves reading, the cinema, music, laughing with her friends, and looking at the sea. She also enjoys walking in the countryside in England and Spain, and one day she hopes to walk the Camino de Santiago in northern Spain. Lesley has also written *V is for Vampire*, *Lisa's Song*, *Deep Trouble*, and *The Real McCoy and Other Ghost Stories*, and has adapted *Twenty Thousand Leagues under the Sea* and *The Secret Agent* in the Dominoes series. She likes watching old horror movies.

OXFORD
UNIVERSITY PRESS

Story Characters

Professor Clark

Tasha Kiara

*Chaz,
a TV reporter*

*Leroy,
a TV camera operator*

*Ella,
a TV sound engineer*

*Sam,
a tanker truck driver*

Zombies

Police officers

Contents

BEFORE READING

1 **Match the words and pictures. Use a dictionary to help you.**

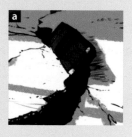

1 cemetery

2 earthquake

3 lab

4 rats

5 scientist

6 zombies

2 **What do you think happens in the story? Complete the sentences with the words from Activity 1.**

a Professor Clark is an American . . . .

b He works in a . . . . in the town of Brillo.

c He works with white . . . .

d One day, a big . . . . hits the town.

e Dead people in the . . . . are suddenly alive again.

f A lot of . . . . come after Professor Clark.

CHAPTER 1
In the Professor's lab

Professor Clark is an important **scientist** in the United States. Day and night, he works in his **lab**. It's in the hills near the little town of Brillo in California.

He's working on a new **serum**. 'This can change everything!' he thinks.

Tasha Kiara is a young scientist in the Professor's lab. She isn't happy about Professor Clark's latest work.

The Professor is always saying, 'Why must people die? My new serum can stop that!'

'This can't be right,' Tasha thinks. 'What's the matter with Professor Clark? Is he going **crazy**?'

professor an important person who studies a lot and teaches

scientist a person who studies the natural world

lab (*short for* **laboratory**) a room where a scientist works

serum liquid that comes from an animal which does not get an illness; it can stop other animals getting ill

crazy not thinking well

One day, Tasha sees something **awful**. The Professor **injects** a dead **rat** with his new serum. Minutes later, the rat begins to move on the lab table. It is suddenly alive again!

'Professor! What are you doing?' Tasha cries.

'Look!' Clark smiles. 'This rat's not dead now. My serum works!'

'You can't do this,' says Tasha more quietly. 'It's wrong, Professor. Do it again, and I must tell someone. I must speak to the **local TV station** about you.'

The Professor laughs. His eyes are crazy.

'Do that,' he says. 'But don't bring any **reporters** here now! Not before I'm ready for them.'

awful very bad

inject to put something into the body of a person or animal

rat an animal like a big mouse

local TV station this makes television programmes for part of the country near you

reporter a person who speaks about things on the TV

2

READING CHECK

Write *Tasha* or *Clark* to complete the sentences.

a .....Clark..... has a new serum.

b .... wants never to die.

c .... is not happy about the serum.

d .... is very happy about the serum.

Professor Clark

e .... does not want to speak to reporters now.

f .... must speak to someone soon.

Tasha Kiara

GUESS WHAT

What happens in the next chapter? Tick two boxes to finish each sentence.

a Tasha …

1 calls the local TV station.

2 kills Professor Clark.

3 meets a reporter.

b In the town, …

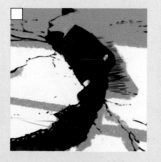

1 there is an earthquake.

2 people run into the street.

3 the zombies arrive.

CHAPTER 2
In the diner

Tasha calls the local TV station. That evening, she meets with the reporter Chaz, his **camera operator** Leroy, and **sound engineer** Ella. They meet in the **diner** in town and talk.

'So, what's the story, Tasha?' Chaz asks.

Tasha tells them all about the Professor, his new serum, and the dead rat.

'Wow!' Ella says. 'That's very interesting!'

'I know,' Tasha answers, 'but it's something **dangerous**, too. Today, it's dead rats. But who knows

camera operator this person takes moving photos for a TV station

sound engineer this person records people talking for a TV station

diner you can eat or drink in this building

dangerous that can kill you

about tomorrow? Professor Clark's work usually helps people, but this is something new. He doesn't listen to me any more. Something's wrong with him.'

'Well, thank you for calling us,' Chaz says. 'It's a wonderful story for our local TV station. But we must go to the lab and speak with the Professor.'

'He's not ready to speak to reporters,' Tasha says, 'but I can open the lab for you. Let's go there tonight. Then you can see the rats and the serum.'

'OK,' Chaz says. 'It's 10 o'clock now. Is this a good time?'

earthquake
when the ground
moves suddenly

'Yes, it is,' Tasha answers. 'The Professor usually goes home at 9.00pm. Hey, what's happening? The table's moving!'

Suddenly, everything in the room is moving. 'Help!' the people in the diner cry.

'It's an **earthquake**!' Leroy says. 'Quick! Let's get out of here!'

They all run into the street.

'Listen. We must go to the lab now!' Tasha tells them. 'There's a lot of serum there. And, with this earthquake, that's dangerous!'

'OK. My car's over there!' Chaz says.

READING CHECK

Are these sentences true or false? Tick the boxes.

		True	False
a	Tasha meets three people from the local TV station.	☑	☐
b	Ella isn't very interested in Tasha's story.	☐	☐
c	Chaz wants to go to the lab.	☐	☐
d	The Professor usually stays at the lab all night.	☐	☐
e	Tasha can open the lab.	☐	☐
f	There is an earthquake when Tasha is in the diner.	☐	☐
g	Tasha is happy about the serum.	☐	☐

GUESS WHAT

What happens in the next chapter? Circle the words to complete the sentences.

a The serum is in the *ground / sky*.

b Some serum goes to the *airport / cemetery*.

c The *zombies / reporters* walk to the lab.

d Professor Clark arrives and asks about *Tasha / his serum*.

e The zombies break the windows of the *lab / supermarket*.

7

CHAPTER 3
From the cemetery

Tasha opens the lab door and goes in. Chaz, Leroy, and Ella go after her.

'Oh, no!' Tasha cries.

The **damage** from the earthquake is very bad. Worst of all, the Professor's new serum is all over the **floor**.

'This isn't good,' Tasha says. 'The serum's in the **ground** under the lab now.'

Ella is looking out through the window at the old **cemetery** not far from the lab. Just then, she gives a sudden cry.

'Look over there! People are coming up out of the ground!' she says.

Tasha goes and looks.

damage when something bad happens to something and it is expensive to make it good again

floor we stand and walk on this in a room

ground we walk on this in the country or the town

cemetery a place where we put dead people under the ground

It is true. Dead people are coming alive.
They are coming from under the ground. Their faces
and their bodies are **grey**. They don't speak, but awful
noises come from their mouths. They move their arms
and legs slowly, and begin to walk from the cemetery
to the lab.

'Those aren't people. They're **zombies**,' Tasha says.
She comes from Haiti, and knows all about zombies.

'Zombies?!' Chaz, Leroy, and Ella cry.

'Yes, and they're coming for us,' Tasha tells them.
'The Professor's serum is doing this. Hungry zombies
eat people's **brains**. Be careful. Don't go near them.
They can **bite** you – and then you change into a
zombie, too!'

grey the colour
between black
and white

zombie a dead
person who
comes alive

brain this is in
your head and you
think with it

bite to cut
something with
your teeth

Suddenly, Professor Clark runs into the lab.

'My serum,' he cries. 'Where is it all?'

'In the ground under the cemetery!' Tasha answers angrily. 'And now a lot of zombies are coming here!'

'That's crazy talk,' the Professor says. 'We're scientists, Tasha. There *are* no Zombies!'

Just then, they hear an awful noise. Someone – or something – is **breaking** the lab windows.

break to make one thing into many little things

10

READING CHECK

Put these sentences in order. Number them 1–6.

a ☐ Professor Clark arrives at the lab.

b ☐ Ella sees the zombies through the window.

c ☐ Professor Clark asks Tasha about his serum.

d ☐ Something breaks the lab windows.

e ☐ Tasha and the TV station people arrive at the lab.

f ☐ The zombies begin to walk away from the cemetery.

GUESS WHAT

What happens in the next chapter? Tick a box to finish each sentence.

a The zombies …

  1 ☐ come for Professor Clark.

  2 ☐ kill Chaz.

  3 ☐ eat all the lab rats.

b Professor Clark …

  1 ☐ watches the zombies interestedly.

  2 ☐ says 'sorry' to Tasha.

  3 ☐ runs away from the zombies.

c Chaz …

  1 ☐ makes friends with the zombies.

  2 ☐ helps Leroy and Ella.

  3 ☐ hits a tree in a car.

d Leroy and Ella …

  1 ☐ drive away in a car.

  2 ☐ are soon zombies.

  3 ☐ bite Tasha.

CHAPTER 4
Through the trees

The next minute, the zombies come through the lab door. They walk slowly over to the Professor. Tasha can **smell** their half-dead bodies.

'Professor Clark, they're coming for you! Quick! You must run!' she cries.

But the Professor is afraid and can't move. The zombies have their hands on him now. Excited noises come from their open mouths.

'You're right, Tasha. Help! They *are* zombies,' he cries. 'I'm sorry, I –'

Suddenly, the zombies **push** the old man to the floor. They **attack** him hungrily, and there is an awful cry.

smell to learn something through your nose

push to move something quickly and strongly with your hands

attack to start hitting someone suddenly; when you start hitting someone suddenly

Leroy and Ella run over to the Professor, but the zombies attack them angrily.

Tasha and Chaz run from the lab and get into Chaz's car. Chaz drives away fast. But it's a dark night, and he can't see well. Suddenly, his car hits a tree. Tasha and Chaz quickly get out, and run through the trees. Far behind them, they hear Leroy and Ella's calls.

'Good. They're OK!' Chaz says. But Tasha looks back. She sees their dead eyes, and their slow walk. Leroy and Ella are zombies now.

'Leave them, Chaz!' she cries.

Chaz and Tasha run back to the road. They see a **tanker truck** on its **side** there. Suddenly, Tasha remembers. Not many things can kill zombies – but **fire** can. They must **burn** the **gas**, and move the zombies into the fire.

Just then, a man with dark **blood** on his face gets up slowly from behind the tanker. He begins walking across to Chaz and Tasha.

'Zombie attack! Run!' Tasha cries.

READING CHECK

Choose the correct words to finish the sentences.

a Professor Clark says sorry because …
  1 the zombies are not very nice. ☐
  2 Tasha is right about the serum. ☑
  3 the rats attack him. ☐

b Tasha and Chaz leave Leroy and Ella because …
  1 they are zombies now. ☐
  2 they are very slow. ☐
  3 they are killing Professor Clark. ☐

c Chaz has an accident because …
  1 his car hits a zombie. ☐
  2 he suddenly feels ill. ☐
  3 he is driving fast and it's dark. ☐

d Tasha knows about zombies because …
  1 she reads a lot. ☐
  2 she comes from Haiti. ☐
  3 she is a zombie. ☐

e Tasha wants to kill the zombies with …
  1 some serum. ☐
  2 her hands. ☐
  3 fire. ☐

GUESS WHAT

What happens in the next chapter? Tick the boxes.

		Yes	No
a	A zombie kills Tasha and Chaz.	☐	☐
b	A man helps Tasha and Chaz.	☐	☐
c	Tasha sees Professor Clark with the zombies.	☐	☐
d	Chaz leaves Tasha with the zombies.	☐	☐
e	The zombies want to attack Chaz and Tasha.	☐	☐
f	The zombies die in a fire.	☐	☐
g	Tasha and Chaz stay alive.	☐	☐

CHAPTER 5
The pool of gas

crash when you hit something and stop suddenly

believe to think something

empty to take everything out of something

'Wait! I'm not a zombie!' the man cries. 'I'm Sam, the driver of this tanker truck. It's on its side now – after my **crash** in the earthquake!'

'Do you **believe** him, Tasha?' Chaz asks.

'I do,' Tasha answers.

Chaz and Tasha go over to the man. Tasha talks about killing the zombies with fire. The two men listen carefully to her.

'Let's do it,' Sam says. 'First, we must **empty** the tanker truck. The more gas the better. Come on! Those zombies aren't far away now!'

Chaz and Tasha help Sam, and the three of them empty the tanker truck. Minutes later, there is a big **pool** of gas all over the road. But there is very little time. The zombies are coming. They are very near the pool now. So Tasha and Chaz must burn the gas quickly – or die!

Sam runs to a **pylon** at the side of the road. Two of its feet are off the ground after the earthquake.

'Let's bring down the **power lines**,' he cries. 'Quick!'

The three of them push over the pylon. It comes down, and it brings the power lines with it.

'Move!' Tasha cries. The power lines hit the pool of gas with a crash!

pool a little liquid on the ground

pylon this tall thing helps to take electricity across the country

power lines electricity goes through these

Whooooosh! Suddenly, there is a very big fire. The sky is red with it, and there is black smoke over everything. The zombies are dying in the fire! Their hair and their coats are burning, and they go down with awful cries. After some time the cries stop, and things go quiet again.

'Hey!' Chaz says. 'The zombies are all dead!'

'Good work!' Tasha cries.

READING CHECK

Use the words in the three fires to write sentences about Chapter 5.

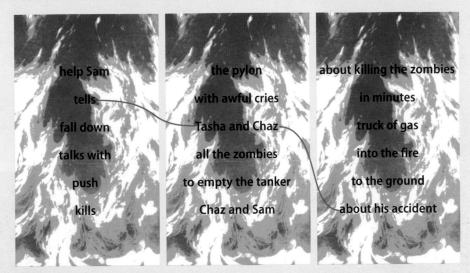

help Sam	the pylon	about killing the zombies
tells	with awful cries	in minutes
fall down	Tasha and Chaz	truck of gas
talks with	all the zombies	into the fire
push	to empty the tanker	to the ground
kills	Chaz and Sam	about his accident

a Sam .. *tells Tasha and Chaz about his accident* ....

b Tasha ....

c Chaz and Tasha ....

d Tasha, Chaz, and Sam ....

e The zombies ....

f The fire ....

GUESS WHAT

**What happens in the next chapter? Choose the words
to complete the sentences.**

a Chaz and Tasha meet at the *cemetery / lab*.

b Tasha is *sorry / happy* about Professor Clark.

c Two *police officers / scientists* come to the lab.

d There is more *gas / serum* at Professor Clark's house.

e Tasha is *happy / not happy* about the latest news.

f Professor Clark is a *zombie / reporter* now.

CHAPTER 6
Bad news

Two weeks later, Chaz is at the lab one morning. He is talking to Tasha.

'Hey, Tasha, how do you feel?' he asks. 'The zombies are all dead now. There's no more dangerous serum here in the lab. You're a **hero**!'

'Not me, Chaz. I'm happy about the zombies, but I'm very sorry for Professor Clark. And your friends Ella and Leroy are dead, too. That's awful.'

'I know. But you and I are OK, and Sam, too.'

Just then, two **police officers** arrive at the lab.

'Ms Kiara, we have some bad **news**,' one of them says.

hero a person who does something important or good

police officer a man or woman who stops people doing bad things

news when someone tells you something new

'What is it?' Tasha asks.

'The earthquake damage all over Brillo is very bad, you know. So we're looking at Professor Clark's house today, and what do we find there?'

'I don't know.'

'A little lab under the house.'

Tasha's face is suddenly white when she hears this. 'A lab, you say?'

'That's right,' the police officer answers. 'And there's more of that serum in it. Maybe there's more serum in the ground there, too.'

'I see,' Tasha says quietly.

Just then, all the people in the room smell something awful – the smell of a dead body. Nobody says a thing. Is this truly happening?

Nobody sees the face at the window – a grey face with blood in its mouth. The zombie is wearing a scientist's white coat. It brings its arms up and it breaks the window with a crash. Professor Clark can't talk or think much now. But he can smell brains – and he's hungry!

READING CHECK

Choose the best answer for each question.

a When do Tasha and Chaz meet again at the lab?

   1 ☐ The next day.

   2 ☐ A year later.

   3 ☑ Two weeks later.

c Where is there more dangerous serum?

   1 ☐ At Professor Clark's house.

   2 ☐ At the police station.

   3 ☐ At the lab.

e What does everyone smell?

   1 ☐ A dirty rat.

   2 ☐ Flowers.

   3 ☐ A dead body.

b How does Tasha feel about Ella and Leroy?

   1 ☐ Happy.

   2 ☐ Bad.

   3 ☐ Angry.

d Why is Tasha's face suddenly white?

   1 ☐ She is ill.

   2 ☐ She is afraid.

   3 ☐ She is cold.

f What does Professor Clark want now?

   1 ☐ Something to eat.

   2 ☐ Some interesting work.

   3 ☐ A talk with Tasha.

GUESS WHAT

What happens after the story ends? Tick the boxes and add your own ideas.

a ☐ Professor Clark bites Chaz.

b ☐ Chaz is soon a zombie.

c ☐ Tasha injects Chaz with a new serum.

d ☐ Chaz dies in Tasha's arms.

e ....

f ....

g ....

Project A *A movie review*

1 Read the movie review. Use a dictionary to help you. Complete the table with notes.

> *The Swarm* is a disaster movie from the year 1978. Its director is Irwin Allen.
>
> The movie is about very big killer bees from Africa. The bees fly across the Atlantic to South America. From there they fly up to Texas in the United States. They kill everything and everybody in front of them. A number of scientists work to stop them.
>
> The movie runs for 116 minutes, and it stars Michael Caine and Katharine Ross.
>
> In my opinion, the movie is very long. The love story in it is not very interesting, and the bees are not very believable. I give it two out of five stars. ★★☆☆☆

Name of movie:	
Type of movie:	
Date:	
Name of director:	
What is the movie about?	
Running time:	
Movie stars:	
Personal star rating:	

2 Read the notes about a different movie.
Use a dictionary to help you.
Complete the review.

Name of movie:	Shaun of the Dead
Type of movie:	Zombie comedy
Date:	2004
Name of director:	Edgar Wright
What is the movie about?	Shaun is 29 years old. He is a bored salesman with a difficult family and girlfriend. When the zombies arrive in town, things are suddenly more interesting for him
Running time:	99 minutes
Movie stars:	Simon Pegg, Nick Frost, and Lucy Davis
Personal star rating:	Four out of five

Shaun of the Dead is a ....
.... from the year .... Its
director is ....
The movie is about a .... -year-old salesman,
Shaun. Shaun is .... His .... and his
.... aren't easy to live with. When the ....
arrive, things are suddenly .... for Shaun.
The movie runs for .... and it stars .... ,
.... , and ....
I like Shaun of the Dead very much. It's a very funny movie. The story moves fast,
and the actors are very good. I give it .... out of ....

3 Find out about a new horror or disaster movie, and write a short review about it.

WORLD WAR Z   THE WOLFMAN   THE THING

CONTAGION   2012   THE HAPPENING

Project B *Interviewing a character*

1 Complete the 'before-the-story-begins' interview with Tasha. Put the reporter's questions in the correct places.

And where are you from?

Do you know a lot about zombies?

So what do you do, Tasha?

Are you the only worker in the lab?

What do you think of Professor Clark?

But do you believe in them?

Reporter: Hello, everyone. This morning, we are talking to Tasha Kiara. Tasha, welcome to *Brillo Today*.

Tasha: Thank you.

Reporter: a) .... ?

Tasha: I work in a lab. I'm a scientist.

Reporter: Right. **b)** .... ?

Tasha: I'm from Haiti.

Reporter: From Haiti! **c)** .... ?

Tasha: I know something. Many people in my country believe in zombies.

Reporter: d) .... ?

Tasha: I don't know. There are some crazy things out there.

Reporter: e) .... ?

Tasha: No, I work with Professor Clark, the famous scientist.

Reporter: f) .... ?

Tasha: He's a wonderful scientist. He works day and night to help people.

2 Complete the 'before-the-story-begins' interview with Chaz. Write answers to the reporter's questions. Use Activity 1 to help you.

from Chicago

is a reporter for the local TV station

knows Tasha — a little

has an open mind — for Chaz, zombies are possible

Professor Clark is a great scientist, Chaz thinks, but a little crazy

Reporter: Our next interview is with Chaz Harper. Hello, Chaz.

Chaz: Hello.

Reporter: Chaz, are you from Brillo?

Chaz: a) ....

Reporter: And do you work in television?

Chaz: b) ....

Reporter: Do you know Tasha Kiara?

Chaz: c) ....

Reporter: What do you think of all these stories about zombies?

Chaz: d) ....

Reporter: What do you think of Professor Clark?

Chaz: e) ....

3 Write three questions for an interview before the story begins with Professor Clark.

Question 1:..

Question 2:..

Question 3:..

4 Imagine you are Professor Clark. Write answers to your three questions in Activity 3.

Answer 1: ....

Answer 2: ....

Answer 3: ....

5 Work in pairs. Role play the interview with your partner.

Student A: You are the Reporter.   Student B: You are Professor Clark.

WORD WORK 1

1 Match the words from Chapters 1 and 2 with the pictures.

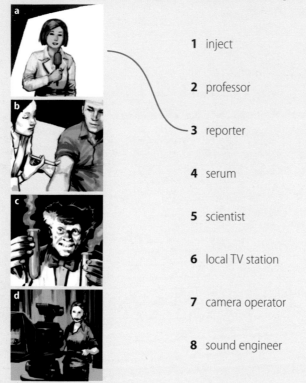

1 inject

2 professor

3 reporter

4 serum

5 scientist

6 local TV station

7 camera operator

8 sound engineer

2 Unscramble the letters in the cars to complete the sentences.

a I'm hungry. Let's go and eat in the d i n e r. NEDRI

b Are there sometimes _ _ _ _ _ _ _ _ _ _ _ _ here? SHAETAQUREK

c That dog is very _ _ _ _ _ _ _ _ _ _. Don't go near it! NARDEGUSO

d This hotel is _ _ _ _ _. I don't want to stay here. WALUF

e My brother is _ _ _ _ _ _. He sleeps in the day and gets up at night. RACYZ

f I can hear noises at night. Are there _ _ _ _ in the house? STAR

g Dr Clark likes working in his _ _ _. ALB

WORD WORK 2

1 Complete each sentence with the best word in the box.

> bites   brain   break   burn   cemetery   ~~damage~~
>
> floor   grey   ground   side   Smell   zombie

a There is often a lot of ...*damage*... after an earthquake.

b You need a good .... to learn quickly and easily.

c Your bag is on the .... under your chair.

d On November 1st, Spanish people take flowers to the .... for the
dead people in their families.

e Let's sit on the .... under that tree. It's out of the sun there.

f Hey! Please don't .... my new phone.

g A .... moves slowly, is half-dead, and can't think very well.

h My dog is very good. He never .... people.

i Today it's cold and the sky is ....

j These flowers are wonderful. .... them!

k Be careful. The milk's very hot now. Don't .... it.

l The car is off the road now and on its ....

2 These words don't match the pictures. Correct them.

a ~~blood~~
...... *fire* ......

b push
....

c fire
....

d attack
....

e tanker truck
....

f gas
....

WORD WORK 3

1 Read the clues and complete the puzzle with new words from Chapter 5.

  a Some water or gas on the ground.

  b To think something.

  c When you hit something and stop.

  d You need these for your TV to work.

  e To take everything out of something.

P O O L

2 What is the name in the dark squares?

  Clue: He works with a camera. _ _ _ _ _

3 Complete each sentence with the best word or phrase in the box.

| hero   news   ~~police officer~~   pylons |

  a A ..*police officer*.. stops people doing bad things.

  b I have some good . . . . for you.

  c The hills have many . . . . across them these days.

  d Tasha is a . . . . because she helps people.

GRAMMAR CHECK

Information questions and question words

We use question words in information questions. We answer these questions by giving some information.

Where is the lab?   *Near Brillo, California.*

Why is Professor Clark happy?   *Because he has a new serum.*

How much serum does Professor Clark have?   *A lot.*

1 Complete the information questions with the question words in the box.

> ~~How many~~ How much What When
> Where Which Who Why

a Q:...How many.....people are with Tasha at the table in the diner?

    A: Three.

b Q:.........................is Tasha angry with Professor Clark?

    A: Because he doesn't listen to her.

c Q:.........................is Sam?

    A: The driver of the tanker truck.

d Q:.........................is the name of the TV reporter?

    A: Chaz.

e Q:.........................town does the earthquake hit?

    A: Brillo.

f Q:.........................time does Tasha have to kill the zombies?

    A: Not much.

g Q:.........................do the zombies come from?

    A: The cemetery.

h Q:.........................do Chaz and Tasha kill the zombies?

    A: After their talk with Sam.

GRAMMAR

GRAMMAR CHECK

Present Simple: *Yes/No* questions and short answers

We use auxiliary verbs or *be* (main verb) in Yes/No questions.

In the short answer, we reuse the auxiliary verb or *be* (main verb).

Do you like zombies?   *No, I don't (do not).*

Are Chaz and Leroy American?   *Yes, they are.*

2 **Write answers for the questions about the people in the story. Use the short answers in the box.**

> Yes, she does.   No, he doesn't.   Yes, they are.
>
> Yes, they do.   No, it isn't.   Yes, he can.   No, she can't.
>
> No, she doesn't.   Yes, he does.   No, they don't.

a Does Tasha live in the United States? ..Yes, she does...........

b Can she stop Professor Clark? ....

c Does she work in a big town? ....

d Does Professor Clark work in a diner? ....

e Does Professor Clark like his work? ....

f Are Chaz and Tasha afraid of the zombies? ....

g Can Chaz help Tasha to kill the zombies? ....

h Is life easy after the earthquake? ....

i Do the zombies kill Tasha? ....

j Do Ella and Leroy go with the zombies? ....

GRAMMAR

GRAMMAR CHECK

Linkers: *and*, *but*, *so*, and *because*

and links two parts of a sentence with the same idea.

Tasha works in a lab, and she helps Professor Clark.

but links two parts of a sentence with different ideas.

Tasha likes lab work, but she doesn't like zombies.

so links two parts of a sentence talking about the result of something.

There is an earthquake so <u>people run into the street</u>.

(result of first part of sentence)

because links two parts of a sentence talking about the reason for something.

Tasha goes to the lab because <u>she wants to see the damage there</u>.

(reason for first part of sentence)

3 Complete the sentences with *and*, *but*, *so*, or *because*.

a Chaz works at a local TV station .... *and* ...... Leroy works there, too.

b Tasha is worried about the Professor .... he works all the time.

c Tasha wants to talk to a reporter .... she phones the local TV station.

d The Professor is a great scientist, ... he is going crazy.

e The zombies attack Professor Clark, ... then they attack Ella and Leroy.

f Sam has an accident .... he has blood on his face.

g Tasha knows about zombies, ... she has a plan to kill them, too.

h Fire kills zombies .... Chaz, Tasha, and Sam bring the power lines down on the pool of gas.

i The zombies die in the fire, ... Professor Clark is not dead.

Dominoes is an enjoyable series of illustrated classic and modern stories in four carefully graded language stages – from Starter to Three – which take learners from beginner to intermediate level.

Each *Domino* reader includes:

- a good story to read and enjoy
- integrated activities to develop reading skills and increase active vocabulary
- personalized projects to make the language and story themes more meaningful
- contextualized grammar practice.

Each *Domino* pack contains a reader, plus a MultiROM with:

- a complete audio recording of the story, fully dramatized to bring it to life
- interactive activities to offer further practice in reading and language skills and to consolidate learning.

If you liked this Quick Starter Level *Domino*, why not read these?

Crying Wolf and Other Tales
Aesop

'Help! A wolf is eating my sheep!'

What happens when a bored shepherd boy lies to the people in his village – or when he later tells the truth?

What do a man and his wife do when their goose lays golden eggs? And what can two travellers learn from a bear in the woods?

These three old Greek tales teach us important truths about people today!

Book ISBN: 978 0 19 424971 3
MultiROM Pack ISBN: 978 0 19 424953 9

Troy
Retold by Bill Bowler

'I see Troy in flames years from now – because Paris brings disaster to us,' says Queen Hecuba about her son.

Paris's father, King Priam, wants to kill him. But Paris lives, and later loves Helen – King Menelaus's queen – from Greece. When Paris brings Helen to Troy, war begins between the Trojans and Greeks.

What happens when Paris's brother Hector, and Greek fighter Achilles, meet in battle? Who wins the war, and how? Read *Troy* and find the answers.

Book ISBN: 978 0 19 424970 6
MultiROM Pack ISBN: 978 0 19 424954 6

You can find details and a full list of books in the Oxford Graded Readers catalogue and Oxford English Language Teaching Catalogue, and on the website: www.oup.com/elt

Teachers: see www.oup.com/elt for a full range of online support, or consult your local office.

	CEFR	Cambridge Exams	IELTS	TOEFL iBT	TOEIC
Level 3	B1	PET	4.0	57-86	550
Level 2	A2–B1	KET-PET	3.0-4.0	–	–
Level 1	A1–A2	YLE Flyers/KET	3.0	–	–
Starter & Quick Starter	A1	YLE Movers	–	–	–